Ultimate

Google

Chrome Bible

The Essential A-Z
Handbook for Everyone

Jerry P. G. Bill

Ultimate Google Chrome Bible

TABLE OF CONTENTS

Introduction to Google Chrome
What is Google Chrome?
Why Choose Chrome?
Installing Chrome on Different Devices
Getting Started with Chrome
Setting Up Your Google Account
Navigating the Chrome Interface
Customizing Your Homepage
Syncing Across Devices
Mastering the Address Bar (Omnibox)
Searching the Web Efficiently
Using Omnibox for Calculations, Weather, and More
Keyboard Shortcuts for Quick Navigation
Tabs and Windows in Google Chrome
Opening, Closing, and Reorganizing Tabs
Managing Multiple Windows
Using Tab Groups for Better Organization
Restoring Accidentally Closed Tabs

Bookmarks and Favorites in Google Chrome
        Creating and Organizing Bookmarks
        Using the Bookmark Manager
        Importing and Exporting Bookmarks
        Bookmark Bar Tips
Chrome Extensions
        What Are Extensions?
        Installing and Managing Extensions
        Recommended Extensions for Beginners and Seniors
        Troubleshooting Extension Issues
Security and Privacy in Google Chrome
        Understanding Chrome's Incognito Mode
        Managing Cookies and Site Data
        Setting Up Safe Browsing
        Password Management and Autofill Features
Customizing Chrome
        Changing Themes and Appearance
        Adjusting Settings for Better Accessibility
        Managing Fonts and Display Sizes
        Configuring Startup Settings
Using Chrome for Productivity
        Leveraging Chrome Profiles for Different Users
        Using Google Workspace Apps in Chrome
        Exploring Chrome's Built-In Tools (e.g., Task Manager, Reader Mode)
Media and Downloads
        Streaming Video and Audio Content

Managing Downloads and File Locations

Casting to Other Devices

Troubleshooting Media Playback Issues

Troubleshooting Common Issues

Clearing Cache and Cookies

Fixing Slow Performance

Resolving Extensions Conflicts

Reporting and Resolving Chrome Crashes

Advanced Features of Google Chrome

Exploring Chrome Flags for Experimental Features

Using Developer Tools

Understanding Chrome Sync Advanced Options

Tips for Faster Browsing

Staying Updated with Google Chrome

Keeping Chrome Updated Automatically

Exploring New Features and Updates

Participating in Beta Testing for Chrome

Benefits of Staying Updated

Chrome on Mobile Devices

Setting Up Chrome on Smartphones and Tablets

Downloading and Installing Chrome

Signing Into Chrome

Syncing Across Devices

Using Chrome Gestures and Voice Search

Chrome Gestures for Navigation

Voice Search

Managing Data Usage on Mobile Chrome

Enabling Lite Mode (Android Only)

Controlling Media Playback

Monitoring Data Usage

Offline Browsing

Additional Tips for Optimizing Chrome on Mobile

FAQs and Quick Reference

Frequently Asked Questions

1. Is Google Chrome Free?

2. Can I Use Chrome Without a Google Account?

3. How Do I Update Google Chrome?

4. What is Incognito Mode, and When Should I Use It?

5. How Do I Restore My Tabs After Chrome Crashes?

6. What Are Chrome Extensions, and Are They Safe?

Cheat Sheet of Chrome Keyboard Shortcuts

Basic Navigation

Search and Navigation

Viewing and Managing Tabs

Zoom and Display

Developer Tools

Common Error Messages and Solutions

1. "Aw, Snap! Something Went Wrong While Displaying This Webpage"

2. "This Site Can't Be Reached"

3. "Your Connection Is Not Private"

4. "ERR_CACHE_MISS"

5. Chrome Won't Open or Crashes

Repeatedly

Glossary of Terms

A

B

C

D

E

F

G

H

I

J

K

L

M

N

O

P

R

S

T

U

V

W

Z

Ultimate Google Chrome Bible

Introduction to Google Chrome

What is Google Chrome?

Google Chrome is a widely-used, high-performance web browser developed by Google. First launched in September 2008, Chrome has grown to become one of the most popular browsers globally, thanks to its speed, security, and simplicity. It enables users to access websites, web applications, and multimedia content online.

Chrome is built on the open-source Chromium project and features a minimalist design aimed at delivering a fast and seamless browsing experience. Its robust performance is attributed to its efficient JavaScript engine, known as V8, and its lightweight design that minimizes memory usage without compromising functionality. Chrome supports various operating systems, including Windows, macOS, Linux, Android, and iOS, making it accessible across a wide range of devices.

Key features of Chrome include:

- A versatile address bar called the Omnibox, which acts as both a search and navigation tool.
- Built-in tools like a password manager, task manager, and download manager.
- Synchronization across devices using a Google Account.
- Compatibility with an extensive library of extensions to enhance productivity and customization.
- A commitment to security, including frequent updates, sandboxing, and built-in phishing and malware protection.

Why Choose Chrome?

There are several compelling reasons why millions of users worldwide prefer Google Chrome over other browsers:

1. **Speed**
   Chrome is renowned for its exceptional speed. It starts quickly, loads web pages faster than many competitors, and delivers a smooth experience even when running multiple tabs or resource-intensive web applications.

2. **User-Friendly Design**
   Its clean and intuitive interface minimizes distractions, making it easy for users of all experience levels, including beginners and seniors, to navigate and perform tasks efficiently.

3. **Cross-Device Synchronization**
   By signing in with a Google Account, users can sync bookmarks, passwords, browsing history, and settings across

multiple devices. This feature is particularly convenient for those who use both desktop and mobile devices.

4. **Security and Privacy**
   Chrome offers built-in protection against phishing, malware, and other online threats. Features like Incognito Mode allow users to browse without saving their history, while frequent updates keep the browser secure against the latest vulnerabilities.

5. **Customization Options**
   Chrome supports a vast collection of extensions, allowing users to personalize their browsing experience. From ad blockers and productivity tools to games and themes, users can tailor Chrome to suit their needs.

6. **Integration with Google Services**
   Chrome integrates seamlessly with Google services like Gmail, Google

Drive, YouTube, and Google Photos, enhancing productivity and convenience.

7. **Regular Updates and Support**
   Google continually updates Chrome to improve performance, introduce new features, and address security concerns, ensuring users have a reliable and cutting-edge browsing experience.

Installing Chrome on Different Devices

Google Chrome can be installed on various devices, including Windows PCs, macOS computers, Android smartphones, and iOS devices. The process is straightforward and typically takes just a few minutes:

1. Installing Chrome on Windows

- Visit the official Google Chrome download page using an existing browser.
- Click the **Download Chrome** button.

- Once the installer is downloaded, double-click the file to start the installation process.
- Follow the on-screen instructions, and Chrome will be installed and set as the default browser if you choose.

2. Installing Chrome on macOS

- Open Safari or another browser and go to the Google Chrome download page.
- Click **Download Chrome** and select the installer compatible with macOS.
- Open the downloaded file and drag the Chrome icon to the Applications folder.
- Launch Chrome from the Applications folder and sign in with your Google Account for full functionality.

3. Installing Chrome on Android Devices

- Open the Google Play Store.
- Search for "Google Chrome" in the search bar.

- Tap the **Install** button next to the Chrome app.
- Once installed, open the app and sign in to sync your data.

4. Installing Chrome on iOS Devices (iPhone and iPad)

- Open the App Store.
- Search for "Google Chrome" in the search field.
- Tap **Get** and authenticate with your Apple ID or Face/Touch ID.
- Once installed, open Chrome and sign in with your Google Account to synchronize settings and data.

Getting Started with Chrome

To fully enjoy the features and benefits of Google Chrome, it's essential to understand its setup and functionality. Let's dive into how you can get started, step-by-step, from creating a Google Account to customizing your browsing experience.

Setting Up Your Google Account

A Google Account unlocks the full potential of Chrome, allowing you to sync data, access Google services, and personalize your experience. Here's how to set one up:

1. Creating a Google Account

- **Visit the Sign-Up Page**: Go to accounts.google.com/signup in your web browser.
- **Fill in the Required Details**: Enter your first and last name, desired email address, password, and confirm the password.
- **Provide Personal Information**: Add your birthdate and gender. This information helps Google tailor services to your needs.
- **Verify Your Phone Number**: For security purposes, Google may ask you to verify your phone number. Enter the code sent to your phone to confirm.
- **Agree to the Terms**: Read through Google's terms of service and privacy policy, then click **I Agree** to create your account.

2. Signing In to Chrome

- Open Chrome on your device.
- Click on the profile icon (a silhouette or circle) in the top-right corner.

- Select **Sign In to Chrome** and enter your Google Account credentials.
- Once signed in, Chrome will sync your bookmarks, browsing history, saved passwords, and other data across devices.

Navigating the Chrome Interface

The Chrome interface is designed to be user-friendly, but knowing its layout ensures a smoother experience. Here's an overview:

1. The Address Bar (Omnibox)

- Located at the top of the browser, the Omnibox functions as both a search bar and a navigation tool.
- You can type in website URLs, search queries, or even perform calculations and look up quick facts.

2. Tabs

- Tabs sit directly below the Omnibox and allow you to open multiple web pages simultaneously.
- Use the + icon to open a new tab, and click the **X** on a tab to close it.
- Right-clicking on a tab reveals options like "Pin Tab" or "Reopen Closed Tab."

3. Menu (Three Dots Icon)

- Found in the top-right corner, this menu gives access to settings, bookmarks, history, and extensions.
- It also provides options for printing, saving pages, or opening new windows.

4. Bookmark Bar

- If enabled, this bar appears below the Omnibox and displays your saved bookmarks for quick access.
- Right-click the bar to organize, rename, or remove bookmarks.

5. Status Bar and Downloads

- The status bar at the bottom shows download progress and file locations.
- Clicking on a completed download opens the file or its folder.

6. Profile Icon

- Clicking this icon lets you switch between Chrome profiles, add new ones, or access guest browsing mode.

Customizing Your Homepage

Your homepage is the first page you see when you open Chrome. Customizing it ensures quick access to your favorite sites.

1. Setting a Specific Homepage

- Click on the three-dot menu in the top-right corner and select **Settings**.
- Scroll down to the **On startup** section.
- Choose one of the following options:

- ○ **Open the New Tab Page**: Displays a default Chrome page with shortcuts to frequently visited sites.
- ○ **Continue Where You Left Off**: Opens the tabs from your last browsing session.
- ○ **Open a Specific Page or Set of Pages**: Enter a URL or multiple URLs for pages you want to load automatically.

2. Adding Shortcuts to the New Tab Page

- Open a new tab and click **Add Shortcut** below the search bar.
- Enter the website's name and URL, then click **Done** to save.

3. Changing Themes

- Go to **Settings** > **Appearance** > **Theme**.
- Browse the Chrome Web Store for themes and select one that suits your preferences.

Syncing Across Devices

One of Chrome's standout features is its ability to sync your data across devices, making it easy to pick up where you left off.

1. What Sync Does

- Sync saves bookmarks, passwords, browsing history, open tabs, and extensions to your Google Account.
- Changes made on one device automatically appear on others where you're signed in.

2. Enabling Sync

- Click on the profile icon in the top-right corner of Chrome.
- Select **Turn On Sync** and sign in with your Google Account.
- Confirm by clicking **Yes, I'm In**.

3. Managing Sync Settings

- Go to **Settings** > **You and Google** > **Sync and Google Services**.
- Choose what you want to sync, such as bookmarks, passwords, or themes. You can also enable **Sync Everything** for a comprehensive experience.

4. Syncing on Mobile Devices

- Open the Chrome app and sign in with your Google Account.
- Go to **Settings** > **Sync** and toggle the features you want to enable.

5. Troubleshooting Sync Issues

- Ensure you're signed in with the same Google Account on all devices.
- Check that sync is enabled in Chrome's settings.
- Update Chrome to the latest version if sync isn't working correctly.

Mastering the Address Bar (Omnibox)

The Omnibox, also known as the address bar, is one of Google Chrome's most versatile and powerful features. Located at the top of your browser, it is more than just a space to type in URLs—it acts as a search engine, a quick calculator, a weather checker, and much more. Mastering the Omnibox can significantly enhance your browsing efficiency and productivity.

Searching the Web Efficiently

One of the primary functions of the Omnibox is searching the web. By understanding how it works, you can retrieve information quickly and effectively.

1. Smart Search Suggestions

- As you type in the Omnibox, Chrome provides real-time suggestions based on your browsing history, bookmarks, and popular search trends.
- Suggestions save time by reducing the need to type full search queries or URLs.

2. Searching with Specific Search Engines

- Chrome allows you to search using different search engines directly from the Omnibox.
- Type the name of the search engine (e.g., "Bing" or "DuckDuckGo") followed by your query. Alternatively, you can manage search engines in **Settings > Search engine > Manage search engines and**

site search to assign custom keywords to specific search engines.

3. Direct Search Commands

- To perform a Google search, simply type your query into the Omnibox and hit Enter.
- For more specific searches, you can include operators like:
  - **site:** - Searches within a specific website. For example, site:example.com Chrome tips.
  - **filetype:** - Searches for specific file types, like filetype:pdf physics notes.
  - **" " (Quotes)** - Searches for exact phrases, e.g., "how to master Chrome".

4. Voice Search

- If your device has a microphone, you can use voice commands by clicking the microphone icon in the Omnibox (on the New Tab page) or on Google's homepage.

- This is especially helpful for hands-free searches or for users who find typing cumbersome.

Using Omnibox for Calculations, Weather, and More

The Omnibox is more than a search tool—it doubles as a multifunctional assistant capable of performing tasks directly.

1. Quick Calculations

- Enter mathematical operations such as 5+7, 50/2, or sqrt(16) directly into the Omnibox.
- Chrome instantly displays the result in the dropdown, eliminating the need for a calculator.

2. Checking Weather

- Type "weather" followed by a city name (e.g., weather New York), and the Omnibox will display current conditions and forecasts.
- This feature is great for quickly planning your day or travel.

3. Currency Conversions

- Convert currencies by typing queries like 50 USD to EUR or 100 GBP to INR.
- Chrome provides the most up-to-date exchange rates powered by Google's search engine.

4. Time Zone Information

- Find the current time in different locations by typing time in [city/country] (e.g., time in Tokyo).
- This feature is especially useful for international meetings or trips.

5. Unit Conversions

- Convert units of measurement directly in the Omnibox, such as 10 km to miles or 200 ml to cups.
- This makes it a handy tool for cooking, science, or travel.

6. Definitions and Translations

- Type define [word] to get the meaning of a word (e.g., define omnibox).
- For translations, type [word] in [language] (e.g., hello in Spanish).

Keyboard Shortcuts for Quick Navigation

Using keyboard shortcuts with the Omnibox can speed up navigation and streamline your workflow.

1. Navigating to a Website

- To quickly enter a URL, type the website name and press Ctrl + Enter (Windows) or Cmd + Enter (Mac). This automatically adds "www." and ".com" to the typed name.

- ○ Example: Typing google and pressing the shortcut navigates to www.google.com.

2. Opening a Search in a New Tab

- Press Alt + Enter (Windows) or Cmd + Enter (Mac) after typing a query to open the search results in a new tab.

3. Cycling Through Suggestions

- Use the Up and Down arrow keys to navigate through the Omnibox's suggestions.
- Press Enter to select your desired result or query.

4. Switching Search Engines

- Type the name of a configured search engine and press Tab to use it for your query.

○ Example: Typing YouTube and pressing Tab lets you search directly within YouTube.

5. Reopening a Recently Closed Tab

- Type part of the page title or URL into the Omnibox to find and reopen recently closed tabs.

6. Launching Chrome Features

- Access Chrome's settings, history, downloads, and bookmarks using commands like:
    ○ chrome://settings - Opens the Settings page.
    ○ chrome://history - Opens browsing history.
    ○ chrome://downloads - Opens downloads.

7. Performing Quick Bookmark Searches

- Type a keyword related to a saved bookmark, and the Omnibox will suggest matching bookmarks.

Tabs and Windows in Google Chrome

Tabs and windows are the foundation of web browsing, allowing you to access multiple websites, tasks, and workflows simultaneously. Mastering their management will enhance your productivity and organization while using Chrome.

Opening, Closing, and Reorganizing Tabs

1. Opening Tabs

- To open a new tab, click the **plus (+)** button to the right of the last tab in the tab bar or press Ctrl + T (Windows) or Cmd + T (Mac).

- Right-click a link and select **"Open link in new tab"** to open the link without leaving your current page. Alternatively, press Ctrl + Click (Windows) or Cmd + Click (Mac) on the link.

2. Closing Tabs

- Close a tab by clicking the **X** on the right side of the tab.
- Use the keyboard shortcut Ctrl + W (Windows) or Cmd + W (Mac) to quickly close the current tab.
- Middle-click (or three-finger click on a touchpad) a tab to close it instantly.

3. Reorganizing Tabs

- Rearrange tabs by clicking and dragging them to a new position on the tab bar.
- Drag a tab out of the tab bar to open it in a new window.

- Combine tabs from different windows by dragging a tab into another window's tab bar.

4. Pinning Tabs

- Pin tabs you frequently use, like email or task management tools, by right-clicking the tab and selecting **"Pin tab"**.
- Pinned tabs are smaller and stay at the beginning of the tab bar, reducing clutter.

Managing Multiple Windows

1. Opening a New Window

- To open a new window, click the Chrome menu (three dots in the top-right corner) and select **"New window"** or press Ctrl + N (Windows) or Cmd + N (Mac).
- Open an incognito window by selecting **"New incognito window"** from the menu or pressing Ctrl + Shift + N (Windows) or Cmd + Shift + N (Mac).

2. Switching Between Windows

- Use Alt + Tab (Windows) or Cmd + Tab (Mac) to cycle through open windows.
- On Chrome OS, swipe up or press the **Overview key** to view all open windows.

3. Splitting Windows

- For multitasking, you can split windows side-by-side by dragging a window to the left or right edge of your screen.

4. Restoring Closed Windows

- If you accidentally close a window, reopen it by pressing Ctrl + Shift + T (Windows) or Cmd + Shift + T (Mac). Chrome restores all the tabs from the last closed window.

Using Tab Groups for Better Organization

Tab Groups allow you to group related tabs together, making it easier to manage and organize multiple tabs.

1. Creating a Tab Group

- Right-click a tab and select **"Add tab to new group"**.
- Assign a name and color to the group for easy identification.

2. Adding Tabs to a Group

- Drag tabs into an existing group.
- Right-click a tab, select **"Add tab to group"**, and choose the desired group.

3. Managing Tab Groups

- Collapse or expand a group by clicking its name or colored circle.
- Move a group by clicking and dragging it along the tab bar.
- To ungroup a tab, right-click it and select **"Remove from group"**.

4. Removing a Tab Group

- Right-click the group name and select **"Ungroup"** to separate the tabs without closing them.
- Close the group entirely by right-clicking and selecting **"Close group"**.

5. Syncing Tab Groups Across Devices

- Ensure you're signed into Chrome and syncing is enabled. Your tab groups will be available on other devices linked to your account.

Restoring Accidentally Closed Tabs

It's easy to accidentally close a tab, but Chrome offers multiple ways to restore them.

1. Reopening the Last Closed Tab

- Press Ctrl + Shift + T (Windows) or Cmd + Shift + T (Mac) to reopen the last closed tab or window.

- Repeat the shortcut to restore multiple recently closed tabs in the order they were closed.

2. Using the History Menu

- Access Chrome's history by clicking the menu (three dots in the top-right corner) and selecting **"History"**.
- View a list of recently closed tabs under **"Recently closed"**. Click a tab to reopen it.

3. Restoring Tabs from a Previous Session

- If you've closed Chrome entirely, relaunch it, and Chrome can restore all tabs from your last session if enabled.
- To ensure this feature works, go to **Settings > On startup** and select **"Continue where you left off."**

4. Syncing Across Devices

- Open tabs from other devices by clicking the Chrome menu, selecting **"History"**, and viewing tabs under the **"Tabs from other devices"** section.

Bookmarks and Favorites in Google Chrome

Bookmarks and favorites are essential tools for saving and organizing your most-visited websites, allowing you to quickly return to important pages without typing URLs repeatedly. In Chrome, bookmarks are user-friendly and feature-rich, making it simple to manage your favorite websites efficiently.

Creating and Organizing Bookmarks

1. Creating a Bookmark

- **From the Omnibox**: When you're on a page you want to save, click the star icon in the Omnibox (address bar).
- A dialog box appears, allowing you to name the bookmark and select the folder where it will be saved.
- Use the shortcut Ctrl + D (Windows) or Cmd + D (Mac) to create a bookmark instantly.

2. Organizing Bookmarks

- Bookmarks can be organized into folders for better navigation:
  - Right-click the **Bookmark Bar** or open the **Bookmark Manager** and select **"Add folder"**.
  - Name the folder and drag bookmarks into it.
- Nest folders within folders to create a hierarchical structure. For example, you can have a folder named "Work" with subfolders like "Projects" and "Research."

3. Renaming and Editing Bookmarks

- Right-click a bookmark and choose **"Edit"** to rename or change the URL.
- Keep names short and descriptive to save space on the Bookmark Bar.

4. Deleting Bookmarks

- To remove a bookmark, right-click it and select **"Delete"**, or open the **Bookmark Manager**, select the bookmark, and press Delete.

Using the Bookmark Manager

The Bookmark Manager is a powerful tool for organizing and maintaining a large number of bookmarks.

1. Accessing the Bookmark Manager

- Click the Chrome menu (three dots in the top-right corner), navigate to **Bookmarks**, and select **"Bookmark manager"**.

- Use the shortcut Ctrl + Shift + O (Windows) or Cmd + Option + B (Mac) to open it directly.

2. Features of the Bookmark Manager

- **Drag and Drop**: Rearrange bookmarks by dragging them to a new position or folder.
- **Search Bar**: Use the search bar at the top of the Bookmark Manager to quickly locate a bookmark.
- **Sorting Options**: Right-click a folder and select **"Sort by name"** to arrange bookmarks alphabetically.

3. Managing Folders

- Create new folders or subfolders by clicking the three-dot menu in the Bookmark Manager and selecting **"Add new folder."**
- Drag and drop folders to reorganize your bookmark structure.

4. Bulk Operations

italic>Ultimate Google Chrome Bible</em>

- Select multiple bookmarks by holding down Ctrl (Windows) or Cmd (Mac) and clicking on the desired bookmarks. Perform actions like moving or deleting them as a group.

Importing and Exporting Bookmarks

Chrome allows you to import bookmarks from other browsers or export your bookmarks for use elsewhere or as a backup.

1. Importing Bookmarks

- Open the Bookmark Manager (Ctrl + Shift + O or Cmd + Option + B).
- Click the three-dot menu in the top-right corner and select **"Import bookmarks."**
- Choose the file to import or select the browser from which you want to import bookmarks. Chrome supports imports from HTML files or directly from other browsers installed on your system.

2. Exporting Bookmarks

- In the Bookmark Manager, click the three-dot menu and select **"Export bookmarks."**
- Chrome saves all bookmarks as an HTML file that you can import into another browser or use as a backup.

3. Syncing Bookmarks

- If you use Chrome on multiple devices, enabling sync ensures your bookmarks are accessible everywhere. Go to **Settings > You and Google > Sync and Google services**, and toggle on **Bookmarks**.

Bookmark Bar Tips

The Bookmark Bar is a highly visible and quick-access location for your most important bookmarks.

1. Displaying the Bookmark Bar

- To show or hide the Bookmark Bar, use the shortcut Ctrl + Shift + B (Windows) or Cmd + Shift + B (Mac).
- Alternatively, go to **Settings > Appearance** and toggle **"Show bookmarks bar"** on or off.

2. Maximizing Space

- Keep bookmark names short or remove the names entirely to display only the website's icon (favicon). Right-click a bookmark, select **"Edit"**, and clear the name field.
- Use folders to group bookmarks, saving space on the bar while keeping them accessible.

3. Quick Access Features

- Drag bookmarks or folders into the Bookmark Bar for faster access.
- Right-click a folder in the bar and select **"Open all"** to open all bookmarks in that folder in separate tabs.

4. Using the Bookmark Bar Context Menu

- Right-click the bar for options like adding folders, pasting URLs, or accessing the Bookmark Manager.

Chrome Extensions

Chrome extensions are small software programs designed to enhance the functionality of Google Chrome. They allow users to customize their browsing experience, streamline workflows, and add features that aren't built into the browser by default. For beginners and seniors, extensions can make browsing more accessible, secure, and enjoyable.

What Are Extensions?

Definition: Extensions are add-ons installed within Chrome to perform specific functions or enhance existing ones. Think of them as tools that let you tailor Chrome to meet your needs, whether for productivity, accessibility, or entertainment.

Examples of What Extensions Can Do:

- Block ads on websites.
- Translate text into different languages.
- Manage passwords securely.
- Provide weather updates directly in the browser.
- Enhance accessibility with features like text-to-speech or zoom controls.

Extensions are available through the Chrome Web Store and can be installed with just a few clicks.

Installing and Managing Extensions

1. Installing Extensions

- Open the Chrome Web Store by typing chrome://extensions/ in the address bar or searching for "Chrome Web Store" online.

- Browse or search for the extension you want to install. Popular categories include productivity, security, and accessibility.
- Click on the desired extension and select **"Add to Chrome."**
- A pop-up will appear detailing the permissions the extension needs. Review the permissions, and if you agree, click **"Add extension."**
- Once installed, the extension's icon will appear in the toolbar near the top-right corner of Chrome.

2. Managing Extensions

- **Accessing Extensions**: Click the puzzle-piece icon in the toolbar to see a list of installed extensions. From here, you can pin or unpin extensions to the toolbar for easier access.
- **Enabling/Disabling Extensions**: Go to chrome://extensions/ or click the Chrome menu (three dots in the top-right corner) > **More tools > Extensions.** Use the toggle

switch to enable or disable individual extensions.

- **Removing Extensions**: In the Extensions page (chrome://extensions/), click **Remove** under the extension you want to delete.

3. Configuring Extension Settings

Many extensions have customizable settings:

- Right-click the extension icon in the toolbar and select **"Options"** or **"Settings."**
- Adjust the features according to your needs, such as enabling specific filters in an ad blocker or setting default languages for a translator.

Recommended Extensions for Beginners and Seniors

Here are some beginner-friendly and senior-friendly extensions to improve your browsing experience:

1. Productivity Extensions

- **Evernote Web Clipper**: Save articles, images, and websites to your Evernote account for future reference.
- **Grammarly**: Helps you write error-free emails, messages, and documents.

2. Security Extensions

- **LastPass**: A password manager that stores and auto-fills your passwords securely.
- **HTTPS Everywhere**: Forces websites to use secure connections for safer browsing.

3. Accessibility Extensions

- **Zoom for Chrome**: Easily adjust text and image sizes on any webpage.
- **Read Aloud**: Converts text to speech, ideal for those with vision impairments.

4. Ad Blockers

- **AdBlock**: Blocks intrusive ads for a smoother browsing experience.

- **uBlock Origin**: A lightweight ad blocker that's customizable and effective.

5. Organization Extensions

- **Tab Wrangler**: Automatically closes unused tabs to keep your workspace tidy.
- **Pocket**: Save articles and videos for later viewing.

6. Utility Extensions

- **Google Translate**: Instantly translate text and entire webpages.
- **Checker Plus for Gmail**: Get Gmail notifications and manage emails without opening a new tab.

Troubleshooting Extension Issues

Despite their usefulness, extensions can sometimes cause problems. Here's how to troubleshoot common issues:

1. Extension Not Working Properly

- Ensure the extension is enabled by visiting chrome://extensions/.
- Update the extension: Click **Details** under the extension and check for updates in the Extensions page.
- Check the permissions: Some extensions may need access to specific sites or data to function correctly.

2. Chrome Slows Down or Crashes

- Disable unused extensions: Too many active extensions can slow down your browser.
- Clear your browser cache and cookies, as these can sometimes interfere with extension functionality.
- Test for conflicts: Disable all extensions and enable them one by one to identify the problematic one.

3. Extension Missing from Toolbar

- Click the puzzle-piece icon and pin the extension to the toolbar.

- Ensure the extension is installed and enabled in chrome://extensions/.

4. Unable to Install Extensions

- Make sure you're signed in with a Google account and connected to the internet.
- Check for restrictions: If you're using Chrome in a managed environment (e.g., on a work or school device), certain extensions may be blocked by the administrator.

5. Extension Behaving Suspiciously

- Uninstall the extension immediately if it displays ads unexpectedly or redirects you to unwanted websites.
- Use trusted sources: Always install extensions from the official Chrome Web Store to minimize security risks.

Security and Privacy in Google Chrome

Google Chrome is designed with robust security and privacy features to protect your online experience. These tools help safeguard your personal information, enhance browsing safety, and give you control over your data. By understanding and utilizing these features, you can create a safer and more private browsing environment.

Understanding Chrome's Incognito Mode

What is Incognito Mode?
Incognito Mode is a private browsing feature

that prevents Chrome from saving your
browsing history, cookies, site data, and
information entered in forms during a session.
This mode is ideal for scenarios where you want
to keep your browsing activity private, such as
shopping for a surprise gift or using a shared
device.

How to Open Incognito Mode

1. Click the three-dot menu in the top-right
   corner of Chrome.
2. Select **"New Incognito Window."**
3. Alternatively, use the shortcut:
   - **Windows/Linux**: Ctrl + Shift + N
   - **Mac**: Command + Shift + N

Limitations of Incognito Mode

- Incognito Mode doesn't make you
  invisible online. Your internet service
  provider (ISP), employer, or websites you
  visit can still track your activity.
- Extensions are disabled by default in
  Incognito Mode unless manually allowed.

- Downloads and bookmarks created in this mode are saved even after closing the window.

Managing Cookies and Site Data

What Are Cookies?

Cookies are small pieces of data that websites store on your device to remember information about your visit. They help websites keep you logged in, remember your preferences, and provide personalized content.

Managing Cookies

1. Open Chrome settings: Click the three-dot menu > **"Settings."**
2. Navigate to **"Privacy and security"** > **"Cookies and other site data."**
3. Choose from the following options:
   - **Allow all cookies**: Recommended for seamless browsing.

- ○ **Block third-party cookies**: Limits tracking but might cause issues on some websites.
- ○ **Block all cookies**: Provides maximum privacy but may disrupt website functionality.
4. Clear cookies for specific sites:
   - ○ Click **"See all site data and permissions."**
   - ○ Search for the site and remove its cookies by clicking the trash can icon.

Benefits of Managing Cookies

- Prevents websites from storing excessive or unnecessary data.
- Reduces tracking and improves privacy.
- Helps resolve website performance issues caused by outdated cookies.

Setting Up Safe Browsing

What is Safe Browsing?

Safe Browsing is a security feature that protects you from phishing attacks, malicious websites, and dangerous downloads. It alerts you if a site or file is unsafe and provides options to navigate safely.

Types of Safe Browsing

1. **Enhanced Protection**

   o Provides proactive protection against threats.
   o Warns you about risky sites and downloads.
   o Shares limited data with Google to identify new threats.

2. **Standard Protection**

   o Offers basic protection by alerting you about known threats.

3. **No Protection**

   o Disables Safe Browsing, leaving you vulnerable to online threats.

How to Enable Safe Browsing

1. Go to Chrome settings: Click the three-dot menu > **"Settings."**
2. Navigate to **"Privacy and security"** > **"Security."**
3. Choose your desired Safe Browsing level.

Tips for Staying Safe Online

- Avoid clicking on suspicious links or downloading files from untrusted sources.
- Regularly update Chrome to ensure you have the latest security patches.
- Use a reputable antivirus program alongside Safe Browsing for added protection.

Password Management and Autofill Features

Password Management
Chrome has a built-in password manager that securely stores your passwords and makes it easier to log in to websites.

Key Features

- **Save and Autofill Passwords**: Chrome prompts you to save your login credentials for quick future access.
- **Password Checkup**: Alerts you if your passwords are weak or compromised in a data breach.
- **Sync Across Devices**: Saved passwords are accessible on all devices signed in to your Google account.

How to Use Chrome's Password Manager

1. Go to Chrome settings: Click the three-dot menu > **"Settings."**
2. Navigate to **"Autofill"** > **"Passwords."**
3. Enable **"Offer to save passwords"** and **"Auto sign-in."**
4. View or edit saved passwords by clicking the eye icon (requires device authentication).

Autofill Features

Chrome's Autofill tool simplifies online forms

by automatically filling in saved information, such as addresses, payment details, and phone numbers.

How to Manage Autofill Settings

1. In Chrome settings, navigate to **"Autofill."**
2. Choose **"Addresses and more"** or **"Payment methods."**
3. Add, edit, or delete saved information as needed.

Benefits of Password and Autofill Management

- Saves time by reducing repetitive data entry.
- Enhances security with strong, unique passwords for each site.
- Makes online shopping and form submissions more convenient.

Security Tips for Password Management

- Use strong, unique passwords that include a mix of letters, numbers, and symbols.
- Enable two-factor authentication (2FA) for added security.
- Regularly review and update your saved passwords.

Customizing Chrome

Google Chrome is not just a web browser; it's a versatile tool that can be tailored to fit your preferences. Whether you want to make the browser visually appealing, adjust settings to improve usability, or configure how it starts up, Chrome offers plenty of options to customize your browsing experience.

Changing Themes and Appearance

What Are Chrome Themes?
Themes in Chrome allow you to personalize the appearance of the browser, including the background, toolbar, and tabs. Themes range from simple color changes to artistic designs.

How to Change Themes

1. Open Chrome and click the three-dot menu in the top-right corner.
2. Navigate to **"Settings"** > **"Appearance."**
3. Click **"Theme"** to open the Chrome Web Store.
4. Browse through the available themes.
   - Use filters like categories and ratings to find a theme that suits your style.
5. Click a theme to preview it and select **"Add to Chrome"** to apply.

Customizing Colors

Chrome also allows you to customize the colors of your tabs and toolbar.

1. Open a new tab.
2. Click **"Customize Chrome"** in the bottom-right corner.
3. Select **"Color and Theme"** to choose a color scheme or create your own.

Restoring the Default Theme

If you want to return to the original look:

1. Go to **Settings** > **Appearance.**
2. Click **"Reset to Default"** under the Theme option.

Adjusting Settings for Better Accessibility

Accessibility features in Chrome ensure that everyone, including users with disabilities, can browse the web effectively.

Key Accessibility Features

1. **High Contrast Mode**

   - Use a high-contrast theme to improve visibility for users with visual impairments.
   - Install the **"High Contrast"** Chrome extension for more options.
2. **Screen Reader Support**

   - Chrome works with popular screen readers like JAWS and NVDA to read text aloud for users with visual challenges.

3. **Zoom Settings**

   o Increase or decrease the zoom level for better visibility.
     ▪ Shortcut: Press Ctrl (Windows) or Command (Mac) + + or -.
   o Set a default zoom level in **Settings** > **Appearance** > **Page Zoom.**

4. **Live Captions**

   o Generate captions for audio and video content.
   o Enable it in **Settings** > **Accessibility** > **Live Caption.**

5. **Caret Browsing**

   o Navigate web pages with your keyboard using caret browsing.
   o Press F7 to toggle this feature.

How to Enable Accessibility Features

1. Open **Settings** and scroll to **Accessibility** under the **Advanced** section.
2. Enable features like Live Captions, Screen Reader, or High Contrast as needed.

Managing Fonts and Display Sizes

Chrome allows you to adjust fonts and display sizes to improve readability and suit your preferences.

Changing Font Settings

1. Go to **Settings** > **Appearance.**
2. Under **Font Size**, choose from:
   - Very Small, Small, Medium (default), Large, or Very Large.
3. To customize further, click **"Customize fonts."**
   - Adjust the font style and size for standard text, serif, sans-serif, and fixed-width fonts.

Setting Display Zoom

1. Go to **Settings** > **Appearance.**
2. Under **Page Zoom**, set a default zoom level (e.g., 100%, 125%).

Tips for Better Readability

- Use a sans-serif font for cleaner and more modern text display.
- Increase the font size for better readability on high-resolution screens.

Configuring Startup Settings

Chrome allows you to control what happens when you open the browser, ensuring a seamless start to your browsing session.

Startup Options

1. **Open the New Tab Page**
   - Displays a blank page with shortcuts to frequently visited sites.
2. **Continue Where You Left Off**

- Restores all the tabs from your previous session. This is ideal if you often pick up where you left off.

3. **Open a Specific Set of Pages**
   - Automatically opens your chosen websites. Perfect for frequently accessed sites like email or news pages.

How to Configure Startup Settings

1. Open Chrome and click the three-dot menu.
2. Go to **Settings** > **On Startup.**
3. Select your preferred option:
   - **Open the New Tab Page**
   - **Continue Where You Left Off**
   - **Open a Specific Page or Set of Pages**
     - Click **"Add a New Page"** to enter URLs or **"Use Current Pages"** to set all open tabs as your startup pages.

Tips for Optimal Startup Configuration

- Use "Continue Where You Left Off" if you work on long-term projects or multitask frequently.
- Set a single-page startup (like your email) for a faster load time.

Using Chrome for Productivity

Google Chrome is not just a web browser; it's a powerful productivity tool that integrates with various apps, features, and settings to streamline your tasks. Whether you're managing multiple users, collaborating through Google Workspace apps, or using Chrome's built-in tools for task management, there are plenty of ways to boost your productivity. Here's how you can make the most of Chrome to enhance your efficiency.

Leveraging Chrome Profiles for Different Users

Chrome Profiles allow you to create separate environments within a single browser. This feature is invaluable for managing personal, professional, and family accounts without mixing data, passwords, or settings. It's especially useful for users who share their devices or want to keep different browsing experiences.

What Are Chrome Profiles?

A Chrome Profile is a unique setup for a user, complete with its own browser history, bookmarks, saved passwords, and extensions. Profiles can be switched quickly and easily, keeping your data organized and secure.

Creating a New Profile

1. Open Chrome and click on the profile icon in the top-right corner.
2. Select **"Add"** to create a new profile.
3. You'll be prompted to sign in with a Google account. Signing in syncs your data across devices and ensures a personalized experience.

4. Once created, you can customize each profile with unique themes, extensions, and settings.

Switching Between Profiles

- Click on the profile icon in the top-right corner of Chrome.
- Choose the profile you want to switch to.
- Chrome will load the profile's specific settings, extensions, and bookmarks.

Using Profiles for Different Purposes

- **Personal Profile**: Use it for browsing, managing your personal accounts, and entertainment.
- **Work Profile**: Log into your work email, calendar, and apps. Keep work-related data separate.
- **Guest Profile**: Ideal when someone else uses your device, offering a temporary, non-tracked browsing session.

Benefits of Using Chrome Profiles

- Keep personal and professional browsing separate.
- Access customized bookmarks, extensions, and settings in each profile.
- Sync data across devices without mixing personal accounts.
- Switch quickly between profiles for a seamless experience.

Using Google Workspace Apps in Chrome

Google Workspace (formerly G Suite) is a suite of cloud-based tools that includes apps like Gmail, Google Docs, Google Sheets, Google Drive, and Google Meet. These apps are deeply integrated into Chrome and provide a powerful set of tools for managing your work, collaborating, and staying productive.

Accessing Google Workspace Apps
Google Workspace apps are designed to work seamlessly in Chrome, ensuring fast and

efficient workflows. You can use them directly in the browser or install them for quick access.

1. **Gmail**:

   ○ Manage your email with ease by logging into your Gmail account.
   ○ Use Chrome extensions like **Checker Plus for Gmail** to enhance email management and receive desktop notifications.

2. **Google Docs/Sheets/Slides**:

   ○ Create, edit, and collaborate on documents, spreadsheets, and presentations directly in Chrome.
   ○ Google Docs auto-saves your work, so you never lose a draft.
   ○ Use **voice typing** in Docs for hands-free document creation.

3. **Google Drive**:

- Store and organize all your files on Google Drive, accessible from any device.
- Use Chrome's built-in search capabilities to quickly find documents and other resources in Drive.
- Share files and folders with colleagues or friends, setting permissions for viewing, commenting, or editing.

4. **Google Meet**:

- Conduct video meetings and online collaborations with Google Meet.
- Chrome optimizes Meet's performance, including features like screen sharing and virtual backgrounds.

Using Google Workspace Extensions for Chrome

Google offers a variety of extensions to integrate Workspace apps more seamlessly into your Chrome experience. Some useful extensions include:

- **Google Keep**: Quickly capture notes and reminders that sync across all devices.
- **Google Docs Offline**: Work on your documents even without an internet connection, then sync them once you're back online.
- **Google Calendar**: View your calendar and schedule events directly from Chrome.

Benefits of Using Google Workspace in Chrome

- Real-time collaboration: Google Workspace apps like Docs and Sheets let you and your team work on the same document simultaneously, making collaboration effortless.
- Cross-device sync: Access your documents, emails, and files from any device with Chrome.

- Simple sharing and permissions: Sharing Google Docs, Sheets, and Slides is as easy as sending a link, with customizable permissions.

Exploring Chrome's Built-In Tools (e.g., Task Manager, Reader Mode)

Chrome has several built-in tools that can make browsing and task management more efficient. These tools help monitor your browser's performance, focus on content, and organize your tasks without the need for third-party apps.

1. Chrome Task Manager

The Chrome Task Manager is a hidden gem that lets you monitor all processes and resources used by the browser. It's particularly helpful when troubleshooting slow performance or identifying high-resource tasks.

How to Use Task Manager

1. Click on the three-dot menu in the top-right corner.
2. Select **"More Tools"** > **"Task Manager."**
3. The Task Manager will show all the tabs, extensions, and processes running in Chrome, along with their CPU and memory usage.
4. You can end any process by selecting it and clicking **"End Process."**

Benefits of Task Manager

- Monitor how much memory and CPU each tab and extension uses.
- Identify and close resource-heavy tabs or extensions that slow down browsing.
- Keep Chrome running smoothly by managing active processes.

2. Reader Mode

Chrome's Reader Mode (also known as Reader View) simplifies web pages by removing ads, images, and unnecessary formatting. This feature focuses on the text, providing a distraction-free reading experience.

How to Enable Reader Mode

1. Open Chrome and type chrome://flags in the address bar.
2. Search for **"Reader Mode"** and enable the flag.
3. Restart Chrome to apply the change.
4. Once enabled, you'll see a Reader Mode icon (usually in the address bar) when viewing a web page with readable content. Click it to activate the mode.

Benefits of Reader Mode

- Get rid of distractions like pop-up ads and sidebars.
- Customize the font size and background color for an improved reading experience.
- Improve focus by turning a cluttered web page into a clean, readable format.

3. Chrome's Download and Printing Tools

Chrome also comes with built-in tools that simplify file management and printing tasks.

- **Downloads**: Track your downloads from the toolbar, and manage the folder destination directly within Chrome.
- **Printing**: Use Chrome's native printing options for web pages, documents, and PDFs. Select **"Print"** from the menu or press Ctrl + P (Windows) or Command + P (Mac) for a quick printout.

4. Extensions and Bookmarking

While not strictly built-in, extensions like **Evernote Web Clipper** or **Pocket** are integrated directly into Chrome, allowing you to save web content and access it later for offline reading. These tools can enhance your productivity by organizing and archiving valuable information.

Media and Downloads

Google Chrome is a versatile browser that excels in managing multimedia content, such as streaming video and audio, downloading files, casting media to other devices, and troubleshooting playback issues. Whether you're watching a movie, downloading a file, or streaming music, Chrome offers several built-in tools and features to make your media experience seamless.

Streaming Video and Audio Content

One of the most popular uses for Google Chrome is streaming media, including video and audio. Thanks to its compatibility with various streaming services and its robust support for media formats, Chrome allows you to enjoy online content in high quality.

Streaming Video: Chrome supports a wide range of video formats such as MP4, WebM, and Ogg, and integrates smoothly with streaming platforms like YouTube, Netflix, Hulu, and many others. Here are some tips to get the best experience:

1. **Using YouTube**:
   YouTube is arguably the most popular streaming platform, and Chrome provides an excellent browsing environment for it. Just type "youtube.com" in the address bar or use the YouTube app if you have it installed.

   ○ **Quality Control**: When watching videos, YouTube typically adjusts video quality based on your internet speed. However, you can manually select the quality by clicking on the settings icon (gear icon) and choosing **"Quality"**. Chrome supports high-definition (HD) and even ultra-high-definition (UHD) 4K videos, depending on your device and connection.

- ○ **Subtitles and Captions**: Chrome allows you to enable subtitles and captions for a more accessible viewing experience.

2. **Streaming Services**:

Chrome works effortlessly with streaming services such as Netflix, Disney+, Amazon Prime Video, and Hulu. Simply log into your account, select the content you want to watch, and enjoy uninterrupted streaming.

- ○ **Playback Controls**: Chrome provides fast forward, rewind, and pause/play options for videos on these platforms.
- ○ **Video Quality and Data Usage**: If you're streaming over a mobile network, you can manage data usage by lowering video quality.

Most streaming platforms provide a setting to adjust the streaming resolution.

3. **Chrome's Media Controls**:

   ○ **Media Keys**: On most devices, Chrome works with media keys on your keyboard to pause, play, skip, and adjust the volume of audio or video playing in the browser.

   ○ **Picture-in-Picture (PiP) Mode**: Chrome's Picture-in-Picture feature allows you to watch videos in a small, resizable window while you browse other websites. Simply right-click on a video and select **"Picture in Picture"** to enable this mode.

Streaming Audio: Chrome is also compatible with popular music streaming platforms such as Spotify, Pandora, and Apple Music. You can listen to music directly from the browser or cast it to external speakers.

1. **Using Spotify**:
   Open Spotify's web player by navigating to spotify.com and logging into your account. With Chrome, you can listen to music while browsing other websites, and Chrome even lets you control playback through media keys on your keyboard.

   - **Offline Playback**: While streaming audio in Chrome requires an internet connection, Spotify Premium users can download playlists for offline listening, though this feature is available only in the Spotify app.

2. **Casting Audio to Other Devices**:

   - **Google Cast**: Chrome supports casting audio to Google devices, such as Chromecast, Google Nest speakers, and compatible smart TVs. This allows you to play music or podcasts from your browser on more powerful speakers.

- ○ **Streaming from Chrome**: To cast, click on the three-dot menu in the top-right corner of Chrome, select **"Cast"**, and choose the device you want to cast to.

Managing Downloads and File Locations

Downloading files from the internet is a frequent task for most Chrome users. Chrome provides an intuitive download management system that helps you access your files quickly, choose where to save them, and organize them for later use.

Downloading Files in Chrome

1. **Basic Downloads**:
   When you download a file, Chrome saves it by default in the **Downloads** folder. This includes images, documents, PDFs, and any other file type you may download. Simply click on a download link, and Chrome will handle the rest. The

download will appear in the download bar
at the bottom of the browser window.

2. **Changing Download Location**:
   You can specify where Chrome saves
   your downloaded files:

   ○ Open the Chrome menu (three dots)
     in the top-right corner and go to
     "Settings".
   ○ Scroll down and click on
     "Advanced" to reveal more
     options.
   ○ Under the **"Downloads"** section,
     you'll find the option to **"Change"**
     the location.
   ○ Choose a new folder to save your
     files. You can also opt to ask
     Chrome where to save each file
     before downloading by toggling on
     the **"Ask where to save each file
     before downloading"** option.
3. **Managing and Accessing Downloads**:

- ○ **Download Shelf**: When you download a file, Chrome displays a download bar at the bottom of the browser window. Click on the file in this bar to open it, or select the **"Show in Folder"** option to view its location.
- ○ **Downloads Page**: To access your entire download history, press **Ctrl+J** (Windows/Linux) or **Cmd+J** (Mac) to open the **Downloads** page, where you can see all downloaded files. From here, you can open, delete, or clear all downloads.

4. **Managing File Types**:

   If you download a file type regularly (like PDFs), Chrome can be configured to automatically open certain file types after downloading.

- ○ Navigate to the **Downloads** page.

- Click **"Clear All"** or click on the "Always open files of this type" checkbox next to the file type.

Casting to Other Devices

Chrome allows users to cast media from their browser to compatible devices like Chromecast, smart TVs, or Google Nest speakers. This feature is ideal for enjoying videos, music, and even presentations on bigger screens or with higher-quality audio.

Casting from Chrome

1. **Using Chromecast**:
    - Make sure your Chromecast device is plugged into your TV and powered on.
    - Connect your device (laptop, smartphone, or tablet) to the same Wi-Fi network as your Chromecast.

- ○ In Chrome, click the three-dot menu in the top-right corner and select **"Cast"**.
- ○ Select the device you want to cast to. Chrome will cast the browser tab, and you can enjoy the content on your TV.

2. **Casting Audio**:
   - ○ While casting video, Chrome also supports casting audio, which is great for streaming music and podcasts to external speakers.
   - ○ You can cast audio from services like YouTube or Spotify to Chromecast-enabled devices by following the same process outlined for video casting.

Casting Full Desktop

For more advanced users, Chrome allows you to cast your entire desktop to a compatible device.

1. Open the **Cast** menu.
2. Click on **"Cast desktop"**.

3. Select the screen you want to share, and Chrome will display everything happening on your desktop on the connected device.

Troubleshooting Media Playback Issues

Sometimes, issues with media playback can occur while streaming or playing audio/video content in Chrome. These issues may include buffering, poor video quality, audio lag, or even a blank screen. Here's how to troubleshoot common problems:

1. **Check Your Internet Connection**
    Slow or unstable internet connections can cause videos to buffer or fail to load. Ensure your Wi-Fi or wired connection is stable and fast enough to handle streaming. Try running a speed test to determine if your connection meets the requirements for the content you're trying to stream.

2. **Update Chrome**

   Always ensure that Chrome is up-to-date. New updates often fix bugs and improve media playback. To update Chrome:

   - Go to the Chrome menu > **Help** > **About Google Chrome**.
   - Chrome will automatically check for updates and install them if available.

3. **Disable Extensions**

   Some Chrome extensions (such as ad blockers or media downloaders) can interfere with media playback. To rule out extensions:

   - Disable all extensions by going to the **Extensions** page (type chrome://extensions in the address bar) and toggling them off.
   - Restart Chrome and see if media playback improves.

4. **Clear Cache and Cookies**

   A corrupted cache or cookies can affect

video and audio playback. Clearing your browsing data can help resolve issues.

- o Go to the Chrome menu > **More Tools** > **Clear Browsing Data**.
- o Select **Cached images and files** and **Cookies and other site data**.
- o Click **Clear Data**.

5. **Hardware Acceleration**

Chrome uses hardware acceleration to offload certain tasks to your computer's GPU. However, this feature can cause issues with some media content. To disable hardware acceleration:

- o Go to **Settings** > **Advanced** > **System** and toggle off **"Use hardware acceleration when available"**.

6. **Reinstall Chrome**

If none of the above solutions work, try uninstalling and reinstalling Chrome. This ensures that any corrupt files or settings are reset.

Troubleshooting Common Issues

Google Chrome is one of the most reliable browsers, but like any software, it can occasionally run into issues. Fortunately, many of these problems can be fixed with simple troubleshooting steps. Whether you're dealing with slow performance, extensions conflicts, or a sudden crash, knowing how to resolve these common issues will enhance your browsing experience.

Clearing Cache and Cookies

One of the most common causes of browser issues, such as slow performance, broken pages, or outdated content, is a cluttered cache or corrupted cookies. Chrome stores temporary data in its cache to speed up the loading process of websites, but over time, this data can accumulate and cause problems.

What are Cache and Cookies?

- **Cache**: The cache is a storage area where Chrome saves parts of websites you visit frequently (like images, CSS files, etc.). This helps websites load faster the next time you visit them.
- **Cookies**: Cookies are small files that websites store on your computer to remember your preferences, login details, and browsing habits.

When to Clear Cache and Cookies

Clearing cache and cookies is a good idea if you experience issues like:

- Slow page loading times

- Images or files not displaying correctly
- Errors when logging into websites
- Websites displaying outdated information
- Privacy concerns

How to Clear Cache and Cookies:

1. Open Chrome and click the three-dot menu in the top-right corner.
2. Select **"More Tools"** and then **"Clear browsing data."**
3. In the window that appears, select the time range you want to clear. To clear everything, select **"All time"**.
4. Ensure that both **"Cookies and other site data"** and **"Cached images and files"** are checked.
5. Click **"Clear data"**.

This will remove any stored cookies and cache, potentially resolving issues with website content, slow performance, or errors.

Fixing Slow Performance

Google Chrome can sometimes become slow or unresponsive, especially after prolonged use or with many open tabs. There are several reasons for this, ranging from too many extensions to insufficient system resources. Here's how to troubleshoot slow performance:

1. Close Unnecessary Tabs:

- Having too many open tabs can significantly slow down Chrome's performance. If you notice that Chrome is slowing down, try closing tabs you aren't using.
- **Tab Groups** can be helpful for organizing your open tabs and reducing clutter.

2. Disable Unnecessary Extensions:

Extensions add functionality to Chrome, but too many can slow it down.

- Go to **chrome://extensions** in the address bar to view and manage your extensions.
- Disable any extensions you aren't actively using by toggling them off.

- For extensions you still want to use, check if they have an option to run only on specific websites or limit their background activity.

3. Update Chrome:

Running an outdated version of Chrome can cause performance issues. To check for updates:

- Click the three dots in the top-right corner of Chrome and select **"Help"** > **"About Google Chrome."**
- Chrome will automatically check for updates and install them if available.

4. Manage System Resources:

- **Task Manager**: Chrome has its own Task Manager, which shows how much memory each tab and extension is using. To open it, press **Shift+Esc** or go to the Chrome menu > **More Tools** > **Task Manager**.

- Close tabs or extensions that are consuming excessive memory or CPU resources.

5. Hardware Acceleration:

Sometimes, hardware acceleration can cause Chrome to slow down, especially on older computers or with certain video content. To disable it:

- Go to **Settings** > **Advanced** > **System**, and toggle off **"Use hardware acceleration when available."**

6. Clear Cache and Cookies:

As mentioned earlier, clearing cache and cookies can improve Chrome's performance by removing outdated data and improving page load times.

7. Reset Chrome Settings:

If nothing works, you can try resetting Chrome to its default settings. This will disable extensions, clear temporary data, and reset all settings to their original state. To reset:

- Go to **Settings** > **Advanced** > **Reset Settings** > **Restore settings to their original defaults.**

Resolving Extensions Conflicts

Extensions are powerful tools that can enhance Chrome's functionality, but sometimes, one or more extensions can conflict with each other, causing errors or slow performance. Identifying and resolving extension conflicts can help restore Chrome to its optimal performance.

1. Disable All Extensions:

- First, disable all your extensions to see if performance improves.
- Go to **chrome://extensions**, and toggle off all extensions.
- Restart Chrome and see if the issue persists.

2. Enable Extensions One by One:

- If disabling all extensions fixes the issue, enable them one by one, restarting Chrome each time.
- After enabling each extension, check to see if the issue reappears. If it does, the last extension you enabled is likely causing the problem.
- You can then either remove or update the problematic extension.

3. Update Extensions:
Outdated extensions can cause conflicts with Chrome or other extensions. To update:

- Open **chrome://extensions**.
- Enable **Developer mode** at the top-right.
- Click **Update** to automatically update all extensions.

4. Check for Extension Compatibility:
Not all extensions are compatible with each other. For example, two different ad blockers might conflict with each other. Read the extension's description and reviews for

compatibility information, or contact the developer if you suspect a compatibility issue.

5. Reset Chrome to Default Settings:
 If troubleshooting extensions doesn't solve the issue, you can reset Chrome as described in the previous section to disable all extensions and return Chrome to its default state.

Reporting and Resolving Chrome Crashes

Occasionally, Chrome may crash or freeze unexpectedly. Crashes can happen for a variety of reasons, such as conflicting software, corrupted files, or insufficient system resources. Here's how to handle Chrome crashes:

1. Identify the Cause of the Crash:

- **Check for Error Messages**: If Chrome crashes and displays an error message (like **"Aw, Snap!"** or **"Chrome has stopped working"**), note the message, as it can give you clues about the cause of the crash.

- **Check System Resource Usage**: If your computer is running low on memory or CPU power, it may cause Chrome to crash. Try closing other applications or upgrading your system resources.

2. Relaunch Chrome in Incognito Mode:

- If Chrome crashes frequently when browsing certain sites, try opening it in **Incognito Mode** (Ctrl+Shift+N) to see if the problem persists. Since Incognito Mode disables extensions, it can help you determine if an extension is causing the issue.

3. Disable Hardware Acceleration:

- As mentioned earlier, hardware acceleration can sometimes cause crashes in Chrome. Disable it by going to **Settings** > **Advanced** > **System** and toggling off

"Use hardware acceleration when available."

4. Update Chrome and Extensions:

- Outdated versions of Chrome or extensions can cause stability issues. Ensure that both Chrome and your extensions are up to date.

5. Clear Browsing Data:

- Corrupted browsing data, such as cache or cookies, can cause Chrome to crash. To clear browsing data:
  - Go to **Settings** > **Privacy and security** > **Clear browsing data**.
  - Select **All time** and check **Cookies and other site data** and **Cached images and files**, then click **Clear data**.

6. Disable or Remove Problematic Extensions:

- Extensions are often the root cause of crashes. Disable all extensions and see if Chrome still crashes. Then, enable them one by one to pinpoint the problematic extension.

7. Report the Crash to Google:

- If Chrome continues to crash after troubleshooting, you can report the issue directly to Google. When Chrome crashes, it will often prompt you to send a report. You can also go to **chrome://crashes** and submit the crash data.
- You can also search Google's support forums to see if others have reported similar issues and find potential solutions.

8. Reinstall Chrome:

- If all else fails, reinstalling Chrome can resolve deep-rooted problems that might be causing crashes. First, uninstall Chrome from your device, then download and reinstall the latest version from the official website.

Advanced Features of Google Chrome

Google Chrome offers a range of advanced features that can take your browsing experience to the next level. From experimenting with cutting-edge tools to optimizing performance, these advanced capabilities make Chrome a powerful and versatile browser.

Exploring Chrome Flags for Experimental Features

What Are Chrome Flags?
Chrome Flags are experimental features hidden within Chrome that allow users to test new

functionalities before they are officially released. These features are in development and might not always be stable, but they can significantly enhance your browsing experience when used properly.

Accessing Chrome Flags:

1. Open Chrome and type chrome://flags in the address bar.
2. Press **Enter** to view the Flags menu.
3. Use the search bar at the top of the page to find specific features or scroll through the list.

Enabling and Disabling Flags:

- To enable a feature, click the dropdown menu next to it and select **"Enabled."**
- To disable a feature, select **"Disabled."**
- After making changes, click **"Relaunch"** at the bottom of the page to restart Chrome and apply the changes.

Popular Chrome Flags to Try:

1. **Parallel Downloading:** Speeds up downloads by splitting files into smaller chunks downloaded simultaneously.
2. **Smooth Scrolling:** Enhances scrolling experience by making it smoother, especially on pages with heavy content.
3. **Force Dark Mode for Web Contents:** Applies a dark mode to all websites, regardless of whether they support it natively.
4. **Tab Hover Cards:** Displays a preview image of a tab when you hover over it.
5. **Reading Mode:** Provides a clutter-free view of webpages, ideal for reading long articles.

Caution:

Since Chrome Flags are experimental, they can sometimes cause issues like instability or slower performance. If you encounter problems, disable the problematic Flag and restart Chrome.

Using Developer Tools

What Are Developer Tools?

Chrome's Developer Tools (DevTools) are built-in features designed for developers to debug, optimize, and enhance web applications. However, even non-developers can use these tools for advanced troubleshooting and learning more about how websites work.

Accessing Developer Tools:

- Press **Ctrl+Shift+I** (Windows) or **Cmd+Option+I** (Mac).
- Right-click anywhere on a webpage and select **"Inspect."**

Key Features of DevTools:

1. **Elements Tab:**

    - Lets you view and edit the HTML and CSS of a webpage in real time.
    - You can modify text, adjust styles, and experiment with layouts.

2. **Console Tab:**

- Useful for troubleshooting errors on a webpage.
- Displays error messages, warnings, and logs, making it easier to identify issues.

3. **Network Tab:**

- Tracks all network requests made by the webpage.
- Helps diagnose slow-loading pages by identifying large files or slow servers.

4. **Performance Tab:**

- Analyzes the performance of a webpage.
- Useful for identifying elements that slow down loading times or affect responsiveness.

5. **Application Tab:**

- Manages data like cookies, local storage, and session storage used by the website.

Using DevTools for Non-Developers:

- **Troubleshooting Layout Issues:** If a webpage doesn't display correctly, use the **Elements** tab to inspect the layout and experiment with changes.
- **Checking Page Speed:** Use the **Network** tab to identify which files are slowing down the page.
- **Testing Website Responsiveness:** Toggle the device toolbar in DevTools to simulate how a webpage looks on different devices and screen sizes.

Understanding Chrome Sync Advanced Options

What Is Chrome Sync?
 Chrome Sync is a feature that allows you to save and synchronize your bookmarks, history, passwords, and settings across multiple devices. Advanced sync options let you customize which data gets synchronized.

Accessing Sync Settings:

1. Open Chrome and click the three-dot menu in the top-right corner.
2. Go to **Settings > You and Google > Sync and Google services.**
3. Click **"Manage what you sync."**

Advanced Sync Options:

1. **Sync Everything:** Automatically synchronizes all data, including bookmarks, passwords, extensions, and open tabs.
2. **Customize Sync:** Allows you to select specific items to sync, such as:
   - **Bookmarks:** Keeps your bookmarks consistent across devices.
   - **Passwords:** Saves and autofills passwords across devices.
   - **History:** Synchronizes browsing history, making it easy to continue where you left off on another device.

- **Open Tabs:** Enables seamless browsing by syncing active tabs between devices.
- **Extensions:** Ensures that extensions installed on one device are available on others.

Benefits of Chrome Sync:

- Access bookmarks and passwords from any device.
- Continue browsing on a different device without losing open tabs.
- Maintain a consistent browsing experience across all devices.

Privacy Tip:
If you're concerned about privacy, use **Custom Sync** to exclude sensitive data like passwords or payment methods from being synchronized.

Tips for Faster Browsing

Chrome is designed for speed, but there are ways to make it even faster and more efficient. Here are some practical tips:

1. Enable Preloading of Pages:

- Chrome can preload pages it predicts you'll visit, reducing load times.
- Go to **Settings** > **Privacy and security** > **Cookies and other site data** and enable **"Preload pages for faster browsing and searching."**

2. Manage Extensions:

- Too many extensions can slow down Chrome. Disable or remove extensions you don't need.

3. Close Unnecessary Tabs:

- Each open tab uses system resources. Close tabs you're not using to free up memory and improve performance.

4. Clear Browsing Data Regularly:

- Accumulated cache and cookies can slow down Chrome. Clear these periodically to maintain optimal performance.

5. Use Keyboard Shortcuts:

- Save time by mastering Chrome's keyboard shortcuts, such as:
    - **Ctrl+T:** Open a new tab.
    - **Ctrl+W:** Close the current tab.
    - **Ctrl+Shift+T:** Reopen the last closed tab.

6. Enable Hardware Acceleration:

- If you have a modern computer, enable hardware acceleration for smoother video playback and faster graphics rendering.
- Go to **Settings** > **Advanced** > **System** and enable **"Use hardware acceleration when available."**

7. Use Lite Mode (Mobile):

- On mobile devices, enable Lite Mode to reduce data usage and load pages faster.

- Go to **Settings** > **Lite Mode** and toggle it on.

8. Optimize Chrome Settings:

- Disable unnecessary features like background sync or location tracking in the **Settings** menu to improve speed.

9. Update Chrome Regularly:

- Keep Chrome up to date to benefit from the latest speed improvements and bug fixes.

10. Use the Omnibox Smartly:

- Chrome's address bar (Omnibox) doubles as a search tool. Use it to quickly find websites, calculate math problems, or get real-time weather updates without loading a separate page.

Staying Updated with Google Chrome

Staying updated with the latest version of Google Chrome ensures that you benefit from improved performance, enhanced security, and new features. Google Chrome is designed to update automatically, but there are also ways to explore and participate in its ongoing evolution, such as trying beta versions.

Keeping Chrome Updated Automatically

Google Chrome features an auto-update mechanism that ensures your browser remains up to date without requiring manual intervention.

This feature is designed to keep you protected against security vulnerabilities and provide access to the latest tools and enhancements.

How Chrome Auto-Updates Work:

- Chrome periodically checks for updates in the background.
- When an update is available, Chrome downloads it automatically.
- The update is applied when you restart the browser.

Checking if Chrome Is Updated:

1. Click the three-dot menu in the upper-right corner of the browser.
2. Go to **Help** > **About Google Chrome.**
3. Chrome will check for updates and display your current version.
    - If an update is available, it will begin downloading immediately.
    - After installation, you'll be prompted to relaunch Chrome to apply the update.

Troubleshooting Auto-Updates:
If Chrome isn't updating automatically, consider these steps:

1. **Ensure Stable Internet Connection:** Updates require a working internet connection.
2. **Disable Interfering Software:** Antivirus programs or firewalls can sometimes block updates.
3. **Update Manually:** Download the latest version directly from Google Chrome's official website.

Why Regular Updates Matter:

- **Enhanced Security:** Updates protect against malware, phishing attacks, and newly discovered vulnerabilities.
- **Improved Performance:** Updates often include speed enhancements and resource optimizations.
- **Access to New Features:** Stay ahead with the latest functionalities that improve browsing experiences.

Exploring New Features and Updates

Chrome is constantly evolving, with new features being rolled out regularly to improve usability and functionality. Keeping track of these updates allows you to take full advantage of what Chrome offers.

Where to Learn About New Features:

1. **Chrome Release Notes:**

   - Visit the official Chrome blog or release notes page for details on new features and improvements.
   - Access it at chromereleases.googleblog.com.

2. **Google's Social Media Channels:**

   - Follow Chrome's official accounts on platforms like Twitter and YouTube for announcements and tips.

3. **Tech News Websites:**

   ○ Many tech blogs and websites, such as TechCrunch or The Verge, cover major Chrome updates and features.

Testing and Exploring New Features:

- **Chrome Beta Channel:** Install the Beta version of Chrome to experience features before they are rolled out to the public.
- **Flags for Experimental Features:** Access experimental features via Chrome Flags by visiting chrome://flags. Be cautious as some features might be unstable.

Example of Recent Updates:

1. **Tab Search:** Quickly locate open tabs by typing keywords.
2. **Enhanced Privacy Controls:** Improved settings for managing cookies and site data.

3. **Integrated Screenshot Tool:** Allows you to capture and annotate screenshots directly in Chrome.

Tips for Staying Informed:

- Enable notifications from trusted tech blogs or forums that focus on Chrome updates.
- Subscribe to Google's newsletters or alerts to receive the latest information.

Participating in Beta Testing for Chrome

For users who enjoy being on the cutting edge of technology, participating in Google Chrome's beta testing program offers a unique opportunity to preview and influence upcoming features.

What Is Chrome Beta?

Chrome Beta is a version of the browser where Google tests new features before releasing them to the general public. It provides a sneak peek into future updates and allows users to provide feedback.

Installing Chrome Beta:

1. Visit the Chrome Beta download page.
2. Download and install the Beta version alongside your standard Chrome browser.
   - Chrome Beta runs independently, so it won't interfere with your regular browsing experience.

Why Participate in Beta Testing?

1. **Early Access:** Experience cutting-edge features before they are widely available.
2. **Influence Development:** Provide feedback to Google to help shape the final version.
3. **Stay Ahead:** Gain insights into trends and innovations in browser technology.

Tips for Beta Users:

- **Use Caution:** Since beta versions may have bugs or instability, avoid using them for critical tasks.
- **Provide Feedback:** Use Chrome's built-in feedback tool to report issues or suggest improvements.
  - ○ Access this by clicking **Help** > **Report an issue.**

Alternatives to Beta:

 If you want an even earlier look at features, consider the **Canary Channel**—a version of Chrome updated nightly with the latest experimental changes. Note that Canary is highly unstable and meant for advanced users or developers.

Benefits of Staying Updated

Staying updated ensures that you:

- **Remain Protected:** Cybersecurity threats evolve constantly, and updates guard against the latest risks.

- **Experience Innovation:** Gain access to the newest features that improve productivity and usability.
- **Avoid Compatibility Issues:** Older versions of Chrome might struggle to support modern web technologies.

Chrome on Mobile Devices

Google Chrome is one of the most versatile and powerful web browsers available for mobile devices, offering a seamless browsing experience on smartphones and tablets. Its mobile version mirrors much of the functionality of its desktop counterpart while including unique features tailored for mobile users, such as gesture controls, voice search, and data management tools.

Setting Up Chrome on Smartphones and Tablets

Getting started with Chrome on your mobile device is quick and straightforward.

Downloading and Installing Chrome

1. **Android Devices:**

   ○ Most Android devices come with Chrome pre-installed as the default browser.
   ○ If it's not installed, download it from the Google Play Store by searching for "Google Chrome" and tapping **Install**.

2. **iOS Devices:**

   ○ Open the App Store on your iPhone or iPad.
   ○ Search for "Google Chrome" and tap **Get**, then **Install** to download the app.

3. **Other Platforms:**

   ○ For less common mobile platforms, visit google.com/chrome to see if

Chrome is supported and follow the installation instructions.

Signing Into Chrome

After installation:

1. Open Chrome and tap the three-dot menu (usually in the top-right corner).
2. Select **Settings**, then tap **Sign in to Chrome**.
3. Enter your Google account credentials to synchronize your bookmarks, history, and other preferences across devices.

Syncing Across Devices

Syncing allows you to access your browsing data from anywhere.

- Ensure **Sync** is enabled in Chrome's settings.
- Choose what to sync: bookmarks, passwords, history, open tabs, etc.

- Changes made on one device will automatically reflect on all your synced devices.

Using Chrome Gestures and Voice Search

The mobile version of Chrome includes intuitive gestures and voice search to make browsing more convenient.

Chrome Gestures for Navigation

- **Swipe to Navigate:** Swipe left or right across the screen to move backward or forward between pages.
- **Pull to Refresh:** Swipe down from the top of a webpage to refresh the page.
- **Tab Switching:** Swipe horizontally across the address bar to switch between open tabs.
- **Close Tabs Quickly:** On Android, swipe a tab off the screen in the tab overview to close it.

Voice Search

Chrome's voice search feature allows you to perform searches and navigate the web hands-free.

1. Tap the microphone icon in the address bar or on the homepage.
2. Speak your query clearly.
3. Chrome will process your query and display search results or perform the requested action (e.g., "Find the nearest coffee shop").

Tips for Using Voice Search:

- Be specific and concise for better results.
- Use natural language; Chrome's voice recognition is optimized for conversational queries.
- Ensure your device's microphone permissions are enabled for Chrome.

Managing Data Usage on Mobile Chrome

Browsing on mobile devices can quickly consume data, especially when streaming videos or loading media-rich websites. Chrome includes several features to help manage and reduce data usage.

Enabling Lite Mode (Android Only)

Chrome's Lite Mode compresses web pages to reduce data usage while maintaining browsing speed.

1. Open Chrome and go to **Settings** > **Lite Mode**.
2. Toggle it on.

When Lite Mode is active:

- Pages load faster, consuming less data.
- Some high-resolution images or complex scripts may be simplified.

Controlling Media Playback

- **Restrict Autoplay Videos:** Go to Chrome settings and disable autoplay for videos.

- **Lower Video Quality:** Many streaming platforms allow you to adjust video quality to conserve data.

Monitoring Data Usage

1. Access Chrome's **Settings** > **Site settings** > **Data saver reports** to view how much data Lite Mode has saved.
2. Use your device's built-in data usage monitor to track Chrome's consumption.

Offline Browsing

- Save pages for offline reading by tapping the three-dot menu and selecting **Download**.
- Access saved pages anytime under the **Downloads** section.

Additional Tips for Optimizing Chrome on Mobile

1. **Customizing the Homepage:**

   o Set your most visited or favorite
     website as your homepage for quick
     access.

2. **Using Incognito Mode:**

   o For private browsing, tap the
     three-dot menu and select **New
     Incognito Tab**.

3. **Adding to Home Screen:**

   o Save frequently visited websites as
     shortcuts on your device's home
     screen. Tap the three-dot menu and
     select **Add to Home Screen**.

4. **Dark Mode:**

   o Enable Dark Mode for better
     visibility at night and reduced eye
     strain. Go to **Settings** > **Themes** >
     Dark.

5. **Clearing Browsing Data:**

- ○ Regularly clear cookies and cache to maintain speed and privacy. Go to **Settings** > **Privacy and Security** > **Clear Browsing Data**.

FAQs and Quick Reference

This section provides answers to commonly asked questions about Google Chrome, a cheat sheet of essential keyboard shortcuts, and solutions to common error messages. Whether you're a beginner or a seasoned user, this section serves as a handy resource to enhance your Chrome experience.

Frequently Asked Questions

1. Is Google Chrome Free?

Yes, Google Chrome is completely free to download and use on all platforms, including Windows, macOS, Android, and iOS.

2. Can I Use Chrome Without a Google Account?

Yes, you can use Chrome without signing in. However, signing in with a Google account enables features like syncing bookmarks, history, passwords, and extensions across devices.

3. How Do I Update Google Chrome?

Chrome usually updates automatically in the background. To check manually:

- On desktop: Go to the three-dot menu > **Help** > **About Google Chrome**. Chrome will check for updates and install them if available.
- On mobile: Visit the Google Play Store (Android) or App Store (iOS) and check for updates.

4. What is Incognito Mode, and When Should I Use It?

Incognito Mode is a private browsing option that doesn't save your browsing history, cookies, or site data after you close the tab. Use it when:

- Browsing on a shared device.
- Accessing sensitive information like banking.
- Testing how a website behaves for new users.

5. How Do I Restore My Tabs After Chrome Crashes?

If Chrome crashes or closes unexpectedly, reopen it and look for the **Restore Tabs** button at the top of the window. You can also access your recently closed tabs through the three-dot menu > **History**.

6. What Are Chrome Extensions, and Are They Safe?

Chrome extensions are small software programs that enhance functionality. While most are safe, download only from trusted developers via the Chrome Web Store, and always check reviews and permissions before installing.

Cheat Sheet of Chrome Keyboard Shortcuts

Here's a quick reference for commonly used shortcuts to improve your browsing efficiency.

Basic Navigation

- **Open a New Tab:** Ctrl + T (Windows) / Cmd + T (Mac)
- **Close Current Tab:** Ctrl + W / Cmd + W
- **Reopen Last Closed Tab:** Ctrl + Shift + T / Cmd + Shift + T
- **Open a New Window:** Ctrl + N / Cmd + N
- **Switch Between Tabs:** Ctrl + Tab / Cmd + Option + Right Arrow
- **Open Incognito Window:** Ctrl + Shift + N / Cmd + Shift + N

Search and Navigation

- **Search in Current Page:** Ctrl + F / Cmd + F
- **Go to Address Bar:** Ctrl + L / Cmd + L
- **Reload Page:** Ctrl + R / Cmd + R
- **Bookmark Current Page:** Ctrl + D / Cmd + D

Viewing and Managing Tabs

- **Close All Tabs and Exit:** Ctrl + Shift + W / Cmd + Shift + W
- **Open Bookmark Manager:** Ctrl + Shift + O / Cmd + Option + B
- **Open Chrome Task Manager:** Shift + Esc (Windows only)

Zoom and Display

- **Zoom In:** Ctrl + + / Cmd + +
- **Zoom Out:** Ctrl + - / Cmd + -
- **Reset Zoom Level:** Ctrl + 0 / Cmd + 0
- **Toggle Fullscreen:** F11 / Ctrl + Cmd + F

Developer Tools

- **Open Developer Tools:** Ctrl + Shift + I / Cmd + Option + I
- **View Source Code:** Ctrl + U / Cmd + U

Common Error Messages and Solutions

1. "Aw, Snap! Something Went Wrong While Displaying This Webpage"

This error typically occurs due to:

- Low system memory.
- An incompatible extension.
- A corrupted cache.

Solution:

- Reload the page by pressing Ctrl + R / Cmd + R.
- Disable extensions temporarily by going to **Menu > More Tools > Extensions**.
- Clear browsing data (cache and cookies) via **Menu > Settings > Privacy and Security > Clear Browsing Data**.

2. "This Site Can't Be Reached"

This error usually indicates network or DNS issues.

Solution:

- Check your internet connection.
- Restart your router.
- Clear DNS cache by typing chrome://net-internals/#dns in the address bar and clicking **Clear Host Cache**.

3. "Your Connection Is Not Private"

This occurs when Chrome cannot verify the security of a website.

Solution:

- Check the website URL for typos.
- Avoid entering sensitive information if the site is suspicious.
- Proceed only if you trust the site or are using a secure network.

4. "ERR_CACHE_MISS"

This indicates Chrome is unable to retrieve cached data.

Solution:

- Clear your cache via **Menu > Settings > Privacy and Security > Clear Browsing Data**.
- Refresh the page.

5. Chrome Won't Open or Crashes Repeatedly

This can be due to corrupted files, extensions, or outdated versions.

Solution:

- Restart your computer or device.
- Update Chrome to the latest version.
- Reinstall Chrome by uninstalling and downloading it again from the official site.

Glossary of Terms

A

- **Address Bar (Omnibox):** The field at the top of the browser where you can enter web addresses, search queries, or use various Chrome features.
- **Autocomplete:** A feature that suggests web addresses, search queries, or previously visited sites as you type in the address bar.
- **Auto-update:** A process where Chrome automatically downloads and installs updates in the background to ensure you have the latest features and security fixes.

B

- **Bookmark:** A saved shortcut to a webpage, allowing quick access without needing to re-enter the URL.
- **Bookmark Bar:** A toolbar below the address bar that displays your favorite or frequently used bookmarks.
- **Browser:** A software application used to access and display websites on the internet. Google Chrome is an example of a web browser.
- **Browser Cache:** Temporary storage for website data, making websites load faster on subsequent visits.

C

- **Casting:** A feature that lets you display your browser's content on another device, such as a TV, using Google Chromecast.
- **Cookies:** Small pieces of data stored on your device by websites, used to remember preferences or track user activity.

- **Chrome Extensions:** Small software programs that customize and enhance Chrome's functionality.
- **Chrome Flags:** Experimental features in Chrome that can be enabled or disabled by users for advanced customization.
- **Chromium:** An open-source project that serves as the foundation for Google Chrome and other browsers.

D

- **Developer Tools (DevTools):** A set of web development tools built into Chrome, used for debugging and inspecting web pages.
- **Download Manager:** A feature in Chrome that helps manage and organize files downloaded from the internet.
- **DNS (Domain Name System):** A system that translates website names (e.g., www.google.com) into IP addresses.

E

- **Extensions:** See Chrome Extensions.
- **Experimental Features:** Features that are still in testing and may not be fully stable, often accessible through Chrome Flags.

F

- **Favicons:** Small icons that represent websites in browser tabs, bookmarks, and history.
- **Flash Player:** An outdated multimedia software platform that was used for running video, animations, and games on the web. (No longer supported by Chrome.)

G

- **Google Account:** An account used to access Google services, such as Gmail, Google Drive, and Chrome Sync.
- **Google Workspace:** A suite of productivity tools by Google, including Gmail, Google Docs, Sheets, and Drive, which integrate seamlessly with Chrome.

H

- **Homepage:** The first page that opens when you launch Chrome or click the Home button.
- **HTTP (Hypertext Transfer Protocol):** A protocol used for transferring data over the web.
- **HTTPS (Secure HTTP):** A secure version of HTTP that encrypts data for safer browsing.

I

- **Incognito Mode:** A private browsing mode that doesn't save history, cookies, or site data after the session ends.
- **IP Address:** A unique numerical label assigned to each device on a network for identification.

J

- **JavaScript:** A programming language used to create interactive and dynamic content on websites.

K

- **Keyboard Shortcuts:** Key combinations that perform specific tasks quickly within Chrome, such as opening a new tab or refreshing a page.

L

- **Loading Indicator:** A visual cue (usually a spinning circle) showing that a webpage or content is being loaded.

M

- **Malware:** Malicious software designed to harm or exploit devices, which Chrome helps protect against through Safe Browsing.
- **Menu Icon:** The three-dot icon in Chrome's top-right corner, providing access to settings, tools, and other options.

N

- **Navigation Buttons:** Buttons like Back, Forward, and Refresh, used for moving between web pages.
- **Notifications:** Alerts from websites or Chrome extensions that appear in your browser or desktop.

O

- **Omnibox:** See Address Bar.
- **Offline Mode:** A feature that allows certain webpages or apps to be accessed without an internet connection.

P

- **Password Manager:** A built-in tool in Chrome that stores and autofills passwords securely.
- **Phishing:** A type of cyber attack where fraudulent websites try to steal sensitive information like passwords or credit card details. Chrome's Safe Browsing feature helps warn against such sites.

R

- **Reader Mode:** A feature that simplifies web pages by removing ads and distractions for easier reading.
- **Rendering:** The process of displaying web page content in a browser.

S

- **Safe Browsing:** A security feature that protects users from phishing, malware, and other online threats.
- **Search Engine:** A tool used to find information online. Chrome uses Google Search by default but allows customization.
- **Sync:** A feature that links your browsing data (like bookmarks and history) across all devices signed into the same Google account.

T

- **Tab Groups:** A feature that allows users to organize tabs into collapsible groups for better management.

- **Task Manager:** A built-in tool in Chrome that shows active processes and allows you to close unresponsive tabs or extensions.
- **Themes:** Visual designs that change the appearance of Chrome's interface.

U

- **URL (Uniform Resource Locator):** The web address of a specific page or resource on the internet.

V

- **Voice Search:** A feature that lets you perform searches or commands using voice input.

W

- **Web Apps:** Applications that run in a browser and do not require downloading or installation. Examples include Google Docs and Gmail.

- **WebRTC (Web Real-Time Communication):** A technology enabling real-time communication, such as video calls, directly in the browser.

Z

- **Zoom:** A feature to adjust the size of content on a webpage, making it easier to view text and images.

This glossary serves as a comprehensive reference for understanding Google Chrome and its many features. By familiarizing yourself with these terms, you can navigate the browser with greater confidence and efficiency.

www.ingramcontent.com/pod-product-compliance
Lightning Source LLC
Chambersburg PA
CBHW071202050326
40689CB00011B/2214